The Guide to:

Catching Sexual Cheaters

A cheater tells it all

This guide is dedicated to
A family that is supportive
Even to a fallen
Soul

Written by M. J. Archer

Table of Contents

Introduction

I have written this book in order to help stop the moral decay of relationships that is destroying more and more families every day. The downward spiral of morality has compiled its toll on each generation, to the point that our culture is ready to fall. I believe that if we can stop the individuals from cheating on each other, then we can start rebuilding health relationships. Unfortunately, we need to remove the present decay in our relationships by exposing and dealing with the current cheaters among us.

Patterns of life are inescapable facts all around us. How we interact with these conditions, determines how we see, perceive, and live our lives. Each of us has our own unique perspective; we see things in life at different degrees of acceptability. With this tolerance we determine what we can live with and what we can not.

A life of discourse is a normal facet of today's society. Where would we be without the soap operas and reality shows to entertain us on a daily base? Our songs and literature draw our attention by glorifying the affairs of strangers, only to be ignored as someone else's problem. Pornography and minor exposures are all around us, with little notice of how it draws us in. The mind is a raceway that goes unsupervised all day long, hiding in our head desires and dreams. For who can actually read our mind? The intimate thoughts about another that are really behind what we let them see in us.

My warning is up-front and forthcoming; do **not read** this guide if you are not prepared for the truth to be

discovered in your relationships.   Only a minor group of
individuals cheat on their partners, while many have the
thoughts without the action.   It is for you to discover the truth
and the consequence of what you discover for yourself.   I have
no degree in psychology or sociology, but I do have the
experiences and the confessions of many cheaters; that have
been caught.   This guide is a compilation of the major areas
that end up revealing the Cheater.   It is not the only ways or
methods that have been discovered though the life experiences
of friends and loved ones we know.   Every individual cheater
is different in at lest some minor way.   But the fact remains
that they are cheaters and need to stop hurting their partners and
families.   They need to learn that this behavior is not
acceptable.

Psychology of a Cheater

What makes up a cheater? It seems anyone should be able to pick them out in a crowd, or can you? The cheater is not a different race, sex, or group that is easily set apart from others. In fact to look at a cheater, you will find no difference between them and anyone else. The difference is not their **Physical** appearance, but their mental condition.

The mind is where it all begins. A clean mental condition is what we are all born with. As a child grows, images and actions of everything around us begin to imprint on us. Each and every conversation, action, and image; has a role in developing a child's mental outlook.

A cheater is not born, but made. It takes time for the mind to twist and accept that non-conforming way of life. No one sets out to hurt the ones they love. It just becomes the normal way of acceptable life for them. It appears in his or her mind's eye that this is the way everyone is. True or false, in their mind it is true. Do not miss-understand me in saying that cheaters have adapted a new thought pattern than everyone else, or that they are depraved individuals, for that is not the case. Everyone have a degree of non-conforming thought, it is just a matter in which direction it is focused.

The porno's hidden in dad's closet, late night television Shows, the magazines left out at the book store, and thousands of other events that give small imprints on our minds. The permanency of these imprints is strengthened by the person that allows them. Examples; a parent allowing them gives the impression of acceptability, where that of a stranger still has to work its way through our trust and our family standards. Meaning that when a parent, sibling, or friend imprints on us, we accept it a lot easier than if it is done by an outsider.

Acting out the thoughts is a whole new ballpark. To have the thoughts, does not make a person a cheater. Individuals may keep the mind in check by morality, healthy relationships, or a number of other interests that prevent or get in the way of acting out. Some are just to scared or insecure to act out. Remember we can not read the mind of others, and have enough problems figuring out our own, to label them as a cheater.   To qualify as a cheater, you have to cheat.   Not think about cheating, wanting to cheat, or claiming to cheat.   You actually have to be cheating.

Actions that follow are deliberate and to a degree discreet, varying for each cheater individually.   It is easy to see the one that walks up and asks to have sex.   Where the one that manipulates relationships and circumstances over years, is a lot harder to notice.   The following chapters will help to look at parts of the picture instead of the whole picture.   It is easier to hide what is being done when the other person is trying to look at everything, so lets try to look at individual aspects in life to reveal the clues that we just seem not to notice, but are right in front of our face.   With these clues, we find facts; with the facts we pull the proof needed to expose a cheater.

We must remember not to be the influence that makes our faithful partner into a cheater.   We must assume some responsibility for our actions also.   If we push our partners into cheating by our words or actions, then we need to be willing to help draw them back.   We need to be the ones undoing the damage we have contributed to.   I have seen men broken by controlling wives, wives shared by husbands to satisfy sexual desires, and neglected individuals.   Each case resulting in these individuals finding acceptance and love in another's arms. This is a false way to escape the problems in relationships. Escapes that would never been pursued in a healthy relationship.

Another note to consider is how a cheater treats their partner.   A person that is cheating will know that they are doing wrong.   They know that if their partner were cheating on them that they would be offended.   They also try and justify cheating by projecting their partner as being a cheater.   Many cheaters accuse their partners of cheating on them. With or without proof, the cheater knows that they are cheating, and that if they can feel their partner is cheating, then there is nothing wrong with them doing it. It is the ends justify the means. I am cheating because I think you are. They actually feel guilty about themselves and can not accept the responsibility of their own actions. Know every suspicion or action brings an accusation. You know the people I refer to. These are the people that always point the finger and they really need to point it at themselves. When the truth comes out, the accused can actually be madder about the constant accusation than their partner cheating on them. They may have lived for years under the yoke of this oppression, wondering why their partner never trusted them.

Remember if they constantly accuse you of cheating, then they may actually be cheating on you.

Appearance

    Like in the preface I mentioned that cheaters look like everyone else right? To just look at them, this is true. Now lets really LOOK at them. You need to look at your partner intently anyway right? You look at them with love and affection and try to drink them in like a cool glass of water on a hot day. If you do not, then you should. Most couples lose this closeness with time and realize only too late that the spark is gone. Well where did it go?

If you keep looking at your partner, just like you did when you fell in love with them, then it will be harder for them to look away at another.

Now that you understand the intensity of how to look at your partner, open your eyes. Think I am joking? You need to actually see them, not see what you want to see. When you look at them, do you see an insecure individual or a confident one? Will they look you back in the eye, or turn their eyes away? Do they avoid direct contact with you as a normal way of life? You say to your self, it is just the way they are, or you don't understand. Well I do understand.

When Wanda greets her husband at the front door, she waits with open arms. She "sees" that he is not heavy footed as the normal day after work. He closes the car door instead of slamming it. She is relieved that he had a good day at work. When he walks to the front door to meet her, his steps become heavier and his countenance becomes more sullen. He greets her with a passive kiss and says he needs to relax. Wanda asks if he wants chicken for diner or if he wants to go out tonight? He shrugs without looking at her and says it does not matter as he settles down in his recliner to watch whatever is on.

Does this sound familiar to how your partner greets you when they come home? So here is the question, which of you looked at the scene? Wanda noticed he is light hearted when he got out of the car. Why was he light hearted? Did he get a raise, a promotion, maybe a call from an old friend? His being light hearted is nothing to be alarmed at, it is the fact that as he approached **HER,** his light heartedness fades away. His steps become heavier. Now, why would him approaching his wife cause a good day to be not as good? That is where looking at your partner will give you insight. It is only because the presence of his wife has changed his thought process. The question now is what was he thinking about that had him in a good mood to start with? This is the first clue that something good or bad is going on.

Now did the husband look at his wife? Why would I ask that? Well we need to look at our partner to have that intimacy right? His not giving attention or looking at her means he is distracted or does not want to look at her. He shrugs and does not look at her when asked about dinner. Why does he feel she does not deserve the attention that we all give to strangers? Maybe he does not care what he eats, but he should at lest look at her when answering. This shows a lack of respect or even curtsey. So why would he not want to look at his wife? Another clues that they're may be a problem.

Watch how your partner interacts with others. Do they become the social butterflies or do they stay back from the crowd. Neither is wrong, just does it follow suit of the normal routine? Do they act one way with one group of friends and different with another set? Do you see "touches" to arms or legs that seem innocent or are they subtly to get another's attention? A hand on the shoulder is getting attention, the wisp of another's hair is not, and it is flirting. When they look across a room and stare. Did something or someone draw such attention? Watch your partner enough to see signs of longing or affection with others around. Do they whisper in others ears? Whispers are definite signs of breaking personal space. Maybe there is a secret to share or something the do not want spoken aloud. How did the other party respond to the encroachment of personal space? No startle or movement away, even subtle, means that they are familiar with them being in the personal space. Think of how you respond when someone else moves into your space.

Look at them as they leave and as they go. If your partner is a factory worker and leaves in nice clothes instead of the normal work ones, does it not tug at your mind? Are they going to a meeting at work or interview for a promotion? If there is no obvious reason, then there is one that is not meant to be obvious. Did they come home in the same clothes they left in? Most people do not even notice. What story is given for changing clothes? Did they offer it or only explain after you ask? Why are they freshly clean? A manual labor worker you expect to be dirty or smell of sweet. If they now smell like soap, fresh deodorant, or perfume; then you need to ask yourself why, and where did they get clean? If you actually look and see these things, then you need to press them for explanations.

"Hey guys ", Tom said, "you all think you have a great woman, well listen to this. Last night, when I got back from the game, I figured my old lady would be pissed. Well guess what, she met me at the door and almost attacked me. She started by striping off my shirt and rubbing my shoulders. Ah, she said that I was tense, and she wanted to loosen me up. Then she got me out of my clothes and sent me to the shower so I could be clean for dinner. Man it was great; I am the king in my home ".

A mans bragging rights at work. Most of us know what it is like around the break room, the conversations that go on between buddies. Sounds like he had a good time, being greeted so warmly after he was out late. I later learned why his "old Lady" was greeting him so warmly. It was not that she was so great, even though she is, but she was looking his body over to see if there were another woman's markings. She was looking for odd scratches, bruises, lipstick, and so on. She was making sure her territory was not violated by another woman. He never caught on, until he was caught. Thin red streaks on the back and odd lipstick on the thigh, what would you think? After the clues, she pursued the facts, and busted him. She didn't ignore what she found, but addressed it. All because she found a way to look at her man without him knowing.

Clothing

    As mentioned before, clothing with appearance matters. Clothing can hold secrets that we never suspect. It seems so obvious if there is lipstick on the collar, but what about the odd marks? The missing button or the tears in the cuff, some are accidental, but some are evidence that something more is going on.

Like I alluded to before, when your partner wears the wrong type of clothes to work or shows up in a different set, well that should be a definite red flag. Know where your partner says they are going and the clothes they are wearing match. If it is casual Friday one week, it should be the next week. If they are going to church, then they should dress like it. No one wears their good clothes, when they know the clothes will get messed up. I have seen a person that wear worn clothes to a formal event, but that is another issue.

Clothes that are damaged become hard to hide. Neither of you may notice the damage at first glance. Eventually some one will notice that the clothes need to be fixed. It is when odd clothes start showing up or clothes start missing. Where did they come from or where are they going. Some people like to keep "souvenirs" from their conquest. Stains can also give evidence that a person's story is not true. Soy sauce on the shirt when they said lunch was at McDonalds. Since when did McDonalds start to serve Chinese food? Grass stains, blood, sweet stains without reason, and many more; should draw suspicion that needs to be pursued. Use common sense and follow up instead of ignoring facts.

Do you ever wonder why the lint catch has long hair clogging it each week and you both have short hair? So where did it come from? Well I don't know? Pursue the question farther. It has to be coming from some where. Jill finally got so frustrated that she started inspecting all the clothes when she put them in the washer. Long strands of hair are repeatedly found on Tom's sweaters. The fact that she kept finding the hair made her curious. She then confronted him; he told her she was paranoid and crazy. He must be attracting hair by the static electricity caused by the sweater. She bought it, but after

15

a couple more months, she decided to try and figure it out herself.

The hair was driving her nuts, fabric softeners, anti-static sprays, and lint guards, just did not stop the hair from showing up. She now wanted to figure out when and where he was picking it up so she could stop it at the source. The car didn't have hair on the seats, there was no dog, no long hair in the family, and could it be some one he worked with? Well he is a construction worker, so it must be from his work. Some of the construction workers have long hair so it must be from them. She calls his boss and tells him her husband-forgot lunch and she wanted to bring it to him. The boss seemed a little confused, but tells her where his work site is. She can take his lunch to him there.

When she pulled up to the site, the crew was working. Mostly clean cut guys hard at work. She asked the first guy she saw if Tom was around. He said he would look. He came back and told her that Tom was on a supply run. After that he would be checking on another job site. She knows her husband is the foreman, so he has to keep up with big or multiple jobs. She decides to wait for him. She calls the cell phone after an hour and it goes straight to voicemail, just like normal. The same guy comes out and asks her if she wants to leave a message for him, so she doesn't have to wait around. She tells him that she still needs to talk with him. This guy is dirty and greasy, little construction debris on his clothes, like a normal construction worker.

After three hours, a car pulls up and he gets out of the passenger side. It dawns on her that his truck is parked on the side of the building. He carries a little brown bag into the site. He did not even realize her car is parked not far away. She looks over at the car and sees a long hair blond pull away. It slaps her in the face as she realizes where the hair is coming from. She stomps into the site and throws his lunch at him with a couple foul words, and out she goes. She can hear the guys laughing at him, telling him he's been "busted". All because of some hair he kept picking up from a girl friends car, and her also.

Only her irritation about the hair in the lint filter caused her to try and figure it out. She never thought or suspected him seeing some one else. His boss thought he was eating lunch with his wife each day. The crew under him was given excuses as to where he was going. Some knew, but never told, that he was doing more than errands. He was slick, never used his vehicle to see her and didn't try and see her on off work time. He was home when he was supposed to be. Everything seemed air tight with no clues, except for that dam hair in the washer.

Speaking of the washer, have you ever had that partner with those nasty skid marks? Male or female does not matter. Some times females can have them in the front and back. I know what does this have to do with anything, its nasty and gross. Well I will give you credit, it is. Tammy always just sprayed them and went on with the wash. She accepted it as a normal fact of life, don't you? She started to find dried blood near her husbands skids, like why was she looking. Well she has to deal with blood on her own underwear and she recognized it on his. Made her think he had hemorrhoids and just didn't want to mention it. You know a man, talking about that is a sensitive area.

She went and bought some hemorrhoid cream and left it out so he would find it. He did and thought she had bought it for herself. He decided to be helpful and bought some seat cushions so she would be comfortable. She thought he bought them for himself. A lot of assumptions so far, but the occasional blood didn't go away. To top it off he was starting to get a skid in the front of his underwear with blood there also. Now it must be the underwear that is irritating the hemorrhoids, so he must be trying to relieve them by wearing his underwear backwards.

She tells him that he should go and see the doctor about his hemorrhoids. He needs to get them taken care of. He claims he doesn't have them and why did she think he did? Well she didn't want to say it was because she was inspecting his underwear, so she mentions the cream and cushions to him. He still denies them and says he thought she had them. She says she does not. Sound like a soap opera? Well the subject is dropped. She doesn't understand why he will not take care of himself.

She decides to set up a physical for her husband. She tells the nurse to note for the doctor about his hemorrhoids. He doesn't know why he needs a physical. She tells him that he is due for one, because it has been so long. The doctor tells him he is 100% healthy. He just needs to check one more thing. He wants to check his prostate. Well the doctor is sensitive to his patients so instead of wanting to see the hemorrhoids, he wants to check the prostate, something men need done anyway, right? So the doctor gloves up and does the check. He gets an odd look on his face. He asks how long has he had difficulty defecating? The man says he doesn't and why?

The doctor explains that the tears and scares look like some one that is ripping their anus by trying to pass large or hard of feces. So how long has it been going on? The wife assures the doctor that he does not have that problem, but must have hemorrhoids. She points out the blood in the underwear. Doctor looks back and forth at them and decides that he can recommend a marriage counselor for them. Now why do we need a counselor demands the wife, as the husband hangs his head down? The doctor gets up and says he will leave, so they can talk to each other. He lets them use the room. It takes about 2 minutes and the wife storms out crying.

What the hell happened? Some of you figured it out. The man was having an affair, but with men not women. He kept it covered up, but didn't realize that the trauma of anal sex causes rips and bleeding. The stains in the front of his underwear were from not cleaning himself off properly. A little clear sign that was misinterpreted. She would not have thought of him in that way, but the clues were right in front of her for weeks.

The point is that we cannot dismiss the evidence that is on the clothing of our partner, just because we do not want to believe it ourselves. When evidence shows itself, we must see if for what it is. We need to pursue all the possibilities that could be the source of the evidence. Some times it may blow our minds away.

Smell

      The sense of smell is a most under appreciated of the five senses. We appreciate the strong smells, but neglect the more subtle ones all around us. We see movies where detectives and blind people can take the smells of things and determine all sorts of facts that are hidden to our eyes. We also watch animals around us, using their sense of smell to determine the world around them. Without smell, everything in life is altered. Taste, touch, and sight recognition all rely on smell to function properly. You may disagree, so put it to the test.

Plug your nose and close your eyes, let some one else feed you foods at random. Try to determine what they are. Put your hand into different bowls with mixed items, and try to determine what the items are. All your senses work together on a daily base in our perception of the world around us. So why do animals give more attention to smell than even vision? They understand that the sense of smell can determine differences that can not be seen.

When you walk into a kitchen, you can smell the meat cooking, the fresh cut bread, and the cake that was just baked. Some of us go on to smell the burnt residue in the oven, the dirty dishes, and cleaning solution from the floor mopping hours before. But who can take it even further? Can you smell the perfume on your partner's neck at the door, or the mold under the sink? You probably know these are all present, but can you pick out each item's smell?

The level of smell needed to determine what is causing it and the level needed to know there is just an odd smell, are very different. If you can at lest recognize that some smell is bothering you, then you just have to have the initiative to track down the source.

Mark was getting ready for bed in the fall. It was a little chilly, so he started preparing the bed for the night. He kept getting an odd whiff of air that caused him to pause. He recognized that the smell was odd, but what was it? He went to sleep and didn't think much of it. He asked his wife if she could smell something odd. She replied, no. Through out the winter he would catch a whiff of this odd smell, he would stop and try and figure it out. It seems to be coming from the sheets but he was not sure. Was it the fabric softener or the detergent? He knows that his wife changed brands of laundry soap, so he will have to reminder her not to buy it again, he didn't like it. When winter was over and spring came, the smell became less frequent until about May. He found himself in the park, and an intense smell caught his senses. It was the Bradford Pears, the smell that was bothering him in the winter. He hated that smell; it reminded him of the smell that was present with the male orgasm. They had lots of nicknames for this tree, but how did he smell them all winter when the trees didn't have leaves, let alone blossoms? Was it one of the fragrances in the laundry detergent? He got so excited about figuring out the smell, that instead of going back to work after lunch, he went home. Bursting in the door, he yells for his wife and says, "I finally figured out what that smell was." To his surprise, he saw his wife and the neighbor entwined having sex in the livingroom. They were equally surprised.

He actually did just figure out the smell, but it was when he walked in the door. He knew why he didn't like the smell of the tree, and he and his wife were clean about sex, but he did not recognize the orgasm smell of the other man. The smell kept bothering him. He didn't want to acknowledge that it might be devious, but wanted to find another source. So in the winter months his wife and neighbor had sex in the bed where it was warm, and in the warm months, they had sex everywhere else they wanted to. Mark just never came home early. He never thought his buddy next door was over in the day with his wife. He came over on weekends when they watched the ball games. The neighbor would lay in the bed and "snuggle" after sex, so he deposited some of himself on the sheets. This gave the odor that was setting off Mark's sense of smell.

Can you walk in a room and know that a woman is on her monthly cycle? How about when a woman is ovulating? Both times in the month a woman's body will put off different pheromones, that attract men. These pheromones are subtle and hard to recognize, but our bodies still instinctively respond to them. We as men gravitate to women when they ovulate and avoid them when they menstruate. This is the normal cycle of reproduction for the animal species.

A woman can also smell these pheromones from another woman and will respond to them as well. Insecurity and jealousy are two common emotions that evolve when they feel the other woman is visually more appealing than they are. These are more intense when they are menstruating or when the other woman is ovulating. This explains some of the drama between women that does not appear to have a root cause? How many times have we heard, "Its just hormones"? Well in some cases, it is.

When Jane hugged her boyfriend she could sense he was with another woman, so she pushes away in irritation. "You just came from your ex-girlfriend didn't you?" she said.

"No baby", he responds, "what would make you think that. You know how much I hate that crazy woman."

So she then asked, "why do you smell like her then? You know you were just with her and now you come and want to be with me. Why can't you just be true to me?" She slaps him and storms off.

She knew the other girls smell and was not going to let him lie to her. This is a common teenage dating drama that unfolds in the schools everyday. I am sure you remember those days, or try to forget them. People seem more sensitive to another's smell on their date, but they are willing to dismiss it on their spouse. They just don't want to believe it is there. They married me, so they can't be with someone else. These odd smells on a spouse need to be quantified. Is this smell normal to where they say they went, or do the smells not match up?

It is time that we look back to dogs for advice. No not the cheating male, even though I am giving it, but the four legged animals that we call our best friends. They use their nose to great each other. They find out first where the other dog has been before accepting them. We just cannot be as blunt as they are. I say that as a warning, because I actually know of one woman that is. She does not understand why men leave her so quick, but it may be because she literally sniffs their crotch when they come home. They feel invaded and that they are not trusted. She definitely takes things too far.

Work

    The fact is that we all have to work in life.   Work is a necessary evil for most of us.   Some people truly love what they do for a living, while most of us do it for the sake of living. We go day in and day out, back and forth, earning a living for families and ourselves.   An expected facet of adult life that at lest one partner in a couple must do.   Work provides the money needed to survive the everyday needs we have.

What goes on at work, stays at work. This philosophy is common to most of us, but not necessarily true. We come home and talk about co-workers and the problems at work with whoever will listen. We nickname this as venting or winding down. Which means, work does not stay at work. Did you ever think of this philosophy's counter part?

What goes on at home, stays at home. It is the direct counterpart to the work saying. You may laugh because we all know that is never true. We talk about family, with other family, friends, associates, the guy at the bar, and basically anyone that will listen. We definitely talk with the people we work with. The ones we spend roughly 30% of our time with. A little more time than we use to sleep. Dividing the rest of our time between everything else we do in the middle. So you could spend more time with co-workers than you do with your partner. So how does your partner talk about you when they are at work?

Though the years I have experience the basic two conversation about partners at work, the good and the ugly. Either the person loves intently their partner, or they bash their partner. Which do you do? It is a definite sign to everyone that you have a good and stable relationship at home. When you are positive about your partner, everyone knows your relationship is stable. When you are mixed in your comments about them, you appear a realist, a person with normal relationship problems and benefits. When all, or most, is negative; then you show signs of wanting something better or different in life. The underlying tone of discontent shows a need that resonates to most of us.

The negative conversations are a magnet to a cheater, as well as their tool. They can present themselves as unhappy.

They want someone else to step in, with pity, and make themselves feel better. They can also present themselves as the hero that can make another person feel whole. When both methods are combined, the results can be more than they can really handle. By being one's hero or knight in shinning armor; it makes the work place a haven for the other person. When we would rather go to work then stay home, it gives the viewpoint to others that we would rather spend time away from home.

All of these are just conversations and psychological aspects, not physically cheating. The cheating comes on when we act or respond to these situations. A fact that you cannot determine by being away from their work, sorry. Some people just want to be the center of attention. You can only build up suspicion and false jealousy, which fuels the emotional fire. What you can see are signs and facts that your partner is cheating or trying to cheat with someone at work.

"Roberto, Roberto, are you listening to me? Did you realize your boss didn't pay you for your overtime last week? He does this often and you need to confront him. He is just using you and you don't even get paid." She complains.

"Baby, I will take care of it tomorrow." He replies.

"You say that and then it still happens, why can't they fix it the first time. They should just say you are salary if that's what they want you to be, just get a raise to compensate for the hours" she continues to complain.

I have overheard this conversation way to many times. I can see the time clock getting messed up once in a blue moon, or a boss messing up every now and then. I just can not see a business being that incompetent and still having employees. Very poor management or just plan lies? The fact that he didn't come home complaining to her tells me it is a lie. When I work and don't get paid, I get pissed off and angry. I want my money and I want it now. Yes I know I won't get it until the next payday, but I better get it. When your partner does not seem to notice or is not bothered by it, then they know the pay stub is actually correct. They just didn't plan for you to remember how many hours they put in last week. They also do not plan for you to do a good follow up on the matter either. They claim they got it straightened out, but what happened to the money?

Now the way you catch them is simply, you address the work place. If they didn't come to you complaining, then why should you complain to them? It doesn't seem to be bothering them. Call the boss up and ask them if it is true, the hours worked that is. Did they work an extra eight hours Saturday; were they working two hours over on Tuesday and Friday? I guarantee the management has solid records. It is a legal liability that they keep up with it accurately. They will tell you if the time clocks were punched in or out like you were told. They will also tell the worker you called. Tell your partner you were concerned that the pay stub was wrong, but you want their boss to know that you were going to make sure your baby gets paid for the time they worked.

You would be amazed at how many people that cheat are doing it with co-workers. Even when the co-worker knows they are in a relationship. The work place is a playground to attract new partners. Going out afterwards to eat, hanging out in the parking lot after work hours, or spend hours out side of work; all ways to firm up this relationship with each other. The actual affair may start quickly or take a long while to manifest, but the time factor is the basic building block for this relationship. The time differences are the clue that an affair is going on or about to start.

A cheater at work will find away to interact with a potential partner. Even if the person that they are interested in is isolated or a great distance away. The cheater will find a way to make contact. If the person responds politely or warmly, it is up to them. The cheater will find common interest to build a relationship on. These cheaters have no excuses. They intentionally want these affairs. They can not claim being coursed or not being strong enough to resist. These cheaters may even be open about being in a relationship.

The most common story given is that they are getting a divorce. I hear this about may failed relationships. He said he was getting divorced. Did their spouse know that they were getting divorced? People in a divorce will intentionally let their ex-partner know that someone else has come into their life. What better way to say some one else wants me. If some one uses this line to lure you in, then ask to meet the ex-spouse. This bold request that will either confirm the breakup is happening, or will reveal the truth that it is not. You have to be smart enough to pursue this information about a potential partner.

If they are honest, they spent time after work talking with friends or ran an errand. If an errand happened, then where is the item? If they want to spend off-hours with co-workers that are honest relationships, then they should have no problem bringing you along. They may warn you that you will not like the co-workers, but go anyway. Meet the people they are talking about when they come home. If they keep persisting that you are too busy to go, then you really NEED to go. They are playing you as a fool, hoping you don't think they are cheating on you.   But a person this clever will have a backup plan.

When you say you really do want to go and push to go, they will be in a jam, because they expect you to stay home. Plan "B" has to kick in.   Almost every time a phone call "confirming" that the other person is still on for the event has to be made.   In the conversation will be two items, like we talked about and what the event is.   If the plans were made ahead of time, then it is redundant to make this call.   This call is made when the plans were made days or weeks before, not shortly after leaving them at work.   Don't get to paranoid, you have to remember that these are repeated patterns, not one-time events. That pattern should happen every time, not just when you decide to go with your partner.

As a side note, make sure you know where your partner works.   If they work at a set location or if they are mobile.   A person that is mobile has a lot easier time having an affair while on the clock then a person that is expected to be at work at a set time, and set place.   The jokes of the mailman, salesman, and milkman, all started from somewhere.   These cheaters are going to be harder for you to catch, but are a lot more likely to be noticed or caught by someone else.   What you need to hope is that if someone else catches them, then they will at lest tell you about it.

Vehicles

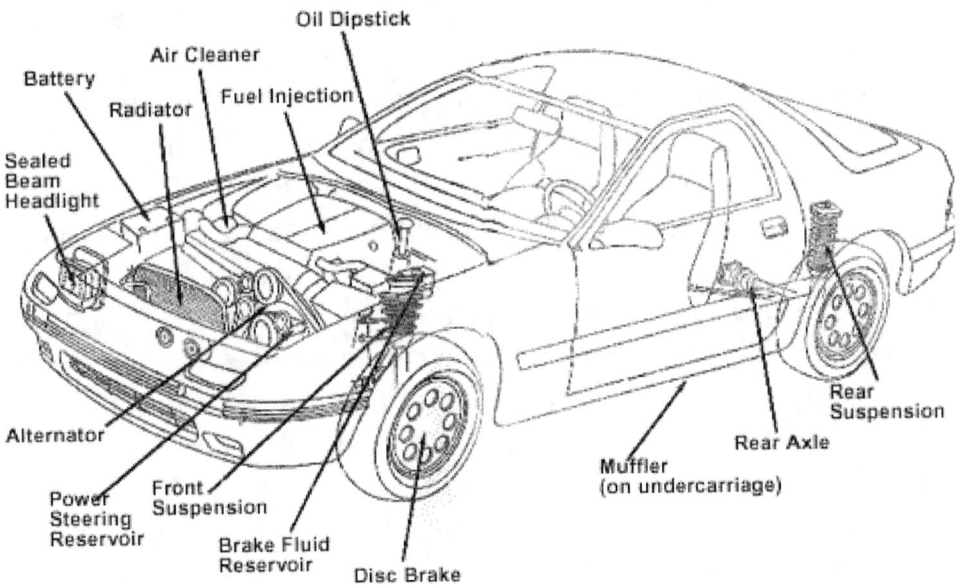

Oil Dipstick

Air Cleaner

Battery

Radiator   Fuel Injection

Sealed
Beam
Headlight

Alternator

Power   Front
Steering Suspension
Reservoir

Brake Fluid
Reservoir   Disc Brake

Muffler
(on undercarriage)

Rear Axle

Rear
Suspension

The way to and from our point A and point B, sometimes
while going by point C, D, and E. The modern way of travel to
work and play. The type of vehicle we drive is an extension of
our personality. It shows others what we think of ourselves.
We do not walk long distances or ride horses anymore. Our
waistlines as a generation shows we would rather get in a car,
then walk down the street. We spend a lot of time in our
vehicles. We need to take the time to "know" what is in our

vehicles.   We also need to know where they have been.

"*Your vehicle is a gas hog Howard.   You should not have to fill it up twice a week.   All you do is drive to work and back.   You might run an errand here or there.   You need to take it in to be serviced or trade it in.   Our last vehicles was the same way and I thought with the new one you wanted, the gas use would go down.*"

Vehicles just use too much gas per mile.   The price of gas goes up and it is digging in to my wallet.   We need to fix this vehicle.   Sound familiar?   How about looking at the odometer and actually see haw much gas is used for how many miles and divided.   This will tell you the miles per gallon. Maybe the fact the car was driven 400 miles in a week is the problem.   This is definitely true when going to work is only 5 miles away.   I mean 5 times to work (10 miles a day), and even two errands to town in the evening (20 more miles a day); adds up to 30 miles a day at 5 day equals 150 miles.   The odometer must be broke.   There is a 250-mile difference.   Either your distances, number of trips, or math is wrong; or someone is making trips you do not know about.

Many companies that have service vehicles use a GPS and locator service on their vehicles.   This lets the serviceperson find places easier and helps employers keep up with employees.   It also helps companies locate stolen goods and missing vehicles.   One company I know also uses the locator as a back up for when the GPS system is wrong.   The service technician can call their dispatch and the dispatcher can lead them over the phone to their destination.   The dispatcher uses the locator map and talks them through.

With the technology in today's culture, you no longer have to follow them or higher someone else to follow them.

Just use the GPS chip in the cell phone and pay for the locator service. Now all you have to do is look on the computer and see a map of where the phone went. The other way is to have a locator chip installed on the vehicle and go through the same process. The chips will not lie. You will find out quickly where all the extra miles are going, with exact locations, so you can visit them at your own convenience.

Vehicles are also the common place for misplaced items. The odd earrings that feel on the floorboard, a note that was discarded, cigarette buts with lipstick, and more end up in the vehicle. The vehicle tells so much about what happens in it. Items found in it can give a lot of insight. The edge of a condom pack in the floorboard is obviously a dead giveaway. The note that was discarded on the floorboard is another. The subtle ones are the different brand of cigarette buts in the ashtray, the odd perfume smell that lingers, the seat adjusted, and etc. Hair on the headrest is one that was mentioned earlier.

A hard one to notice is the finger or hand marks on the inside of the glass. Closed windows and heavy breathing cause condensation on the glass. A handprint on the diver window points to the back of the car, well more than suspicious. Never seen again until the inside of the car is fogged up again. Try it and see.

Just clean the vehicles out on a regular base and it will do two things for you. One, it will help you to be clean, more organized, and feel better about yourself. Two, it will let you find any odd items in the vehicles, that have been misplaced. Look under seats and floor mats for hidden items. The truck and wheel well are good places to hide things for longer periods of time. Above the visor and in the glove box are also areas for small items. Think of all the places that you could hide things in a car. These are the places you need to look. Do not ignore the vehicles. They are the means of transportation for the cheater.

Trips

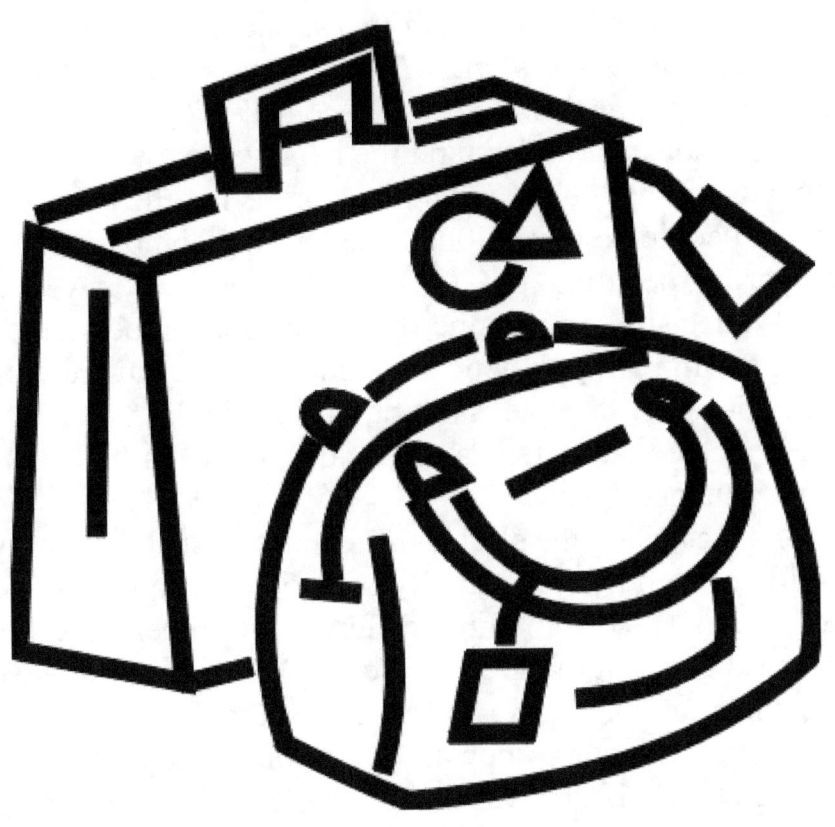

This section goes hand and hand with the last one. The trips made by your partner by car, plane, or train; all have a common theme. They are going somewhere with a purpose, a purpose they have told you about. When your partner deliberately deviates from the planed route, you can bet there is a reason. A cheater will not tell you about this deviation because they do not want you to ask any questions. Usually they did not change their plans to go buy you something, even though this does happen.

Mike complains to his wife, " why does it always take you so long at the store?   Three and four hours for only a couple bags.   I just don't understand why you waste so much time there.   I know when I go with you it doesn't take that long."

Mike does not understand the he gave his own answer and didn't know it.   The time in the store is not the problem.   Yes some people do take a long time, pricing comparing, re-comparing, deciding, put it back, get it back, etc.   A long string of indecision, in just one shopping trip, can be more than frustrating.   In reality they do the same thing if you are with them or not.   The fact she is a lot quicker with him then by herself is a clue that there is a problem.   Knowing this couple, I know the outcome.

She was using the store as an excuse to spend "quality" time with a "friend".   He actually busted her with the phone locator.   He wanted something different for dinner, so called her, since she was at the grocery store.   When her phone went to voicemail automatically, he called the store and had them look for her.   The clerk knew him and confirmed that she came in, but the clerk said she was only there for about ten minutes and left over an hour ago.   He thought the worst; she got in a wreck.   He called 911 dispatch to check is she was in an accident.   No wrecks have been reported.   She still wasn't home either.   He pulls her phone up on the computer and the locator shows she is 4 blocks away.   He decides to drive over and meet her.   He finds her parked at the back of a store, car fogged up, and the car is rocking.   Surprise, surprise; he actually ran his truck into her car.   Yep, a fistfight broke out between him and a naked man.   He sent the other guy to the hospital, the car to the shop, and the marriage to divorce court. They even made the news.   Talk about excitement.

Not everyone is like this.   Some cheat on long distance trips and others don't.   Look at the amount of preparation given for the trips, for these clues.   Where are they going, why are they going, who are they going with.   If they are going to a major city out west and its work related, well what is wrong with that?   Well does their company have a plant out there or a convention?   Is someone else from their work going with them?   Did work buy the plane ticket or supply a per diem sheet to keep up with expenses.   All normal things with a business trip.   Doesn't take a rocket scientist to sort it out. Maybe it's a hunting trip, or a visit to family.   Why can't you go along?   What is the number there so you can call them?   If they are going pheasant hunting, do they own a shotgun?

The Internet has given us the ability to communicate with strangers far away.   It has also given cheaters a larger radius of potential partners.   We all know someone that has ended up in a relationship started online.   Cheaters have been known to take these long trips in order to satisfy their desires.   The risk with these Internet relationships is that someone may just show up at your house that you really did not want there.

"I know you said you were coming here for the weekend to visit our son, but who is she?" Tammy asked.

Tom replies, "This is my new girlfriend, Becky.   Jill and me are getting a divorce.   She is pretty mad about it too.   If she calls, it is just to cuss you out and try to harass me.   She's gone crazy.   Just don't bother answering the phone is she calls".

"Well, I don't know anything about Becky and the car you came in has a Virginia license plate, not a Kentucky one.

So I am not sure if I should let Johnny go with you." Tammy replies.

Tom pleads, "Don't be that way. This is a rental car; mine is in the shop. I am living in Virginia with Becky. You promised me that I could see my son if I came to town. I have a hotel room already. Don't deny me my visitation rights."

Tammy thinks a little and replies, "I will let Johnny spend today and tomorrow with you as agreed, but not the nights. The two of you are not married and we agreed to raise him with good morals. I also want to take a picture of all three of you in front of the car. I want to be able to read the license plate. With these, if you are planning to run off with Johnny, I will have a start point to hunt you down with. Agreed?"

Tom remarks, " Fine, take a picture, I am not stupid enough to run off with him. You would love to find a reason to put me in jail. I will call you this evening to pick him up, but I want him back early in the morning."

Tammy is one smart mom. She does not want to be on the six o'clock news pleading for her sons to be returned. She took the picture for insurance that Tom would not be tempted to go home with Johnny. She now can access through the police all the information he used to rent the car. She has a front photo of all three of them. This shows the newest facial features, clothing they were wearing, and of coarse the vehicle they are using. What she also has is the tool necessary to find out if Tom's story about getting divorced is true or not.

Jill calls that night, as expected, to see if Tom arrived safely. All Tammy asked is "What's going on?" and waits. In a few moments she hears Jill break down in tears. Jill knew that when Tom insisted he go alone, that something was wrong. Tom had told Jill that he was going to a job interview in

Virginia. Since the interview was on Wednesday, he decided it would be a good time to swing over and see his son for the weekend. It was not much further to North Carolina. Tom really went to Virginia to meet an Internet girlfriend. He then was bold enough to bring her on the trip to see his son.

If Tom were smart he would have left the girlfriend at the hotel and should not have mentioned her to his ex-wife. Now his ex-wife has a photo with the new girlfriend standing next to him. Tammy did answer the phone when Jill called. She had been cheated on by Tom before. That's why they got divorced. She suspected that's what he was doing to Jill. The phone conversation confirmed her suspicion and Jill poured her heart out to Tammy. Tammy scanned the photo into the computed and e-mailed it to Jill. Tom never thought Jill would find out. He realized he was busted when he got home and his keys would not open the door. The stupid thing is, he talked Tammy into keeping him.

The point is that you should not be left out of the loop. If it appears things are being withheld, then pursue them. The Internet has taken many online affairs to the point of "trips" to meet each other. We will go over the computer in a later chapter. So stay on the ball and make sure you are filled in about the trip. If they sneak of to a hooker or massage parlor while they are away, you may never know. If you learn the other ways to catch a cheater, then you can still catch them even when they are away.

Phones

      Thanks to modern technology we can walk, drive, work, and play while still having phone access. The cell phone is one of the new necessities of life. Most people feel lost or naked without the cell phone with them. If you own one, you know exactly what I mean. You even expect anyone that you call to pick up, no matter what they are doing. Sometimes you probably wish they didn't answer. And that's why do they think you have to answer them no matter what you are doing? It is more like a technological lease than a helper.

What is not advertised, is that the cell phone is an excellent device to catch a cheater. It provides so much comfort and normalcy to life that a cheater forgets to hide clues it holds. Most of the time they don't bother to try and hind much at all. The feature of pictures, numbers, text, and voicemail; are all good tools for a normal person to communicate with.

Previously I mentioned phone tracking or locators. This feature is automatically built into all new mobile phones. You may need to turn the service on, but the hardware is automatic. The main push for this in the cell phone industry was not to track down your spouse or kids, but to aid in 911 calls. Tracking down the spouse or kids was just a bonus by-product, which they can charge you for. The industry even runs commercials on television for this feature. Buy this product to make sure your children arrive safely at their destinations. Well this is a direct key to map out where the phone goes. The phone is in your partner's pocket. Automatic tracking devices that we carry around and don't even think about.

People used to fear this technology. The fear was that the government wanted to control and track everything about everyone. Maybe they do, but the fact is you want to know where your partner is going also. So turn the feature on and let it transmit where they go. Look it up at your convenience on the computer. You maybe surprise where they go.

The address book and recent call log are the other fun features. Numbers without names that get repeatedly called or received. The name that is on the list a lot that you don't know, and your partner does not mention the call. The listing that is not even a name, but just a letter or odd word, should be in question. These are the group of listings that should concern you.

You can always text them what's up, or how you doing and see what the response is. Just do it from your partner's phone so the other person thinks it's your partner. Call them back and just listen to whom picks up, do they sound familiar? Do they address your partner like they are familiar with them? DON'T talk, it will give you away if there is foul play, just listen. The other side will assume a bad connection. They may call back; just don't answer the phone or hit the ignore button. If the number is innocent or a store, they will give a normal greeting of who they are. They will not sound familiar. You may even recognize the voice.

Text messages are saved in the phone just like a call log, so you can scroll backwards and see who they have been texting. You can also read what the subject matter was. Beware, you may find explicit texting that you may be offended by. You may also find plans to meet at a future time, these you can use to bust your partner with.

Look at stored pictures or pictures they have received. You may find nudes or explicit photos of people you do or do not know. Just remember an explicit photo does not mean they are cheating. Your partner may have a pornography problem. If you find a nude of a child on there, then you have a big problem. This problem will end up in jail time. So take a look at their phone ever now and then, while they do not know you are doing it, just to check up on them. They may already be checking yours without you knowing it.

Pay attention to your partner when they are on the phone. Do they walk away when on the phone? Do they constantly tell the other person they will call them back? Why can they not talk on the phone in front of you? These are all signs that the phone is a tool for secrets, not communicating.

Communication is important in a relationship. The more a relationship is valued directly affects how much communication will be invested. A cheater does not have the ability to spend a lot of time on an affair, so they will utilize the tools they have to keep the communication flowing. Your goal is to find out how your partner is communicating with their new partner and to disrupt it as well as learn from it. You must learn how to communicate again with your own partner. Either to move forward with your relationship, or to glean the information needed to move forward in seperation.

Computers

The computer is a favorite tool for the average family. It is also the favorite tool for scams, and fraud in society. The Police find evidence stored in computers that is key to investigations. So why does the computer play such a big role in our lives, society, and business? It is simple; they have such vast memory. They can store multiple programs to help us work, play, and communicate.   These programs are the keys to the Internet.   They process and store every single thing done on the computer.   Understanding the built in features of these programs gives you the same information pool that investigators use to gather evidence against criminals.

Understanding how to use your computer is essential in your daily life.   Unfortunately, we as individuals think we can figure things out on our own, seeking no formal training.   How long does it take for us to stumble into new knowledge?   We ask one-point learning questions of our friends and co-workers. We try in frustration, not knowing how to get the computer to work for us.   Well, people, it is only a tool.   Now is the time to make it work for you.

Searching your own computer

Looking in your computer is actually pretty easy.   Take and click on the search icon.   Look separately for hidden files, archive files, jpeg's, movie, password protected, and temporary files.   Each search done individually will take time, but will produce lots of information.   After each individual search, look at the titles assigned to each file.   If you know the file or it is a system file, don't bother opening it.   It will slow you down, to like forever, to open each and every file.   Start opening files and scan to see if any thing looks odd.   Watch out for the jpeg's and movie files.   You may see more than you want. Many people keep erotic photos and movie clips in the computer.   It is hard for a sexually deviant person to trash a file that is giving them their fix.   This is especially true when the content is of a person that they desire or are involved with. Have you seen enough already?   When you find the temporary files, you may not actually be able to open all of them. They may be all computer language, that makes no sense to us untrained humans. Instead pay attention to their point of origin. Pull the properties up and see when the file was last accessed or changed. It may be to old to even consider worrying about. You can even write down the IP information and search it out later on the Internet. Remember to look in the little trashcan also. It may not have been emptied in a while.

Where they have gone on the Internet

When you open the Internet, a screen with your home page comes up automatically. This is simple enough to see. What was the last screen up? All you have to do is click the history bar, right? Not always true. The history bar only shows the sites that you go to on your own. It does always show sites that an email or pop-up sends you to. The history can also be edited by users, so it may not show all the sites that have been visited. So yes use the history bar as a reference. See where the last person that used your computer went. See all the sites that have been visited for the last couple of days. The problem is that unless a person is caught off guard, they will clear the history. With a little more time, the Internet function in the control panel lets you clear all the history, clear temp files, clear passwords, and clear bookmarks. So now what do you do to see what is going on when you are not looking?

Lets first ask what and why you want to know. Do you want to see what others are doing online or inside the CPU of your computer? Are you looking to see if there is porn, drug, affair, espionage, or numerous other base issues to worry about? Are you worried that someone else is checking on you? Depending on if you are looking for a specific item or just scanning, everything determines how you will proceed.

Looking for E-mail accounts

To look on line, you have to be online. Just make sure that if you share a computer, that you use the other person's id icon when you start the computer up. This will give you their personalized Internet features. You will go straight to their home page and see their history bar. Yes it will be different than yours. Click on their e-mail site. They may have more than one site. Look for the common ones like Hotmail, AOL, and Yahoo. When you enter one of these sites through their portal, it will prompt an id and password. Just like yours does for you. Click on the id and see if the computer give a choice bar to choose from. Most of them do. Write all the id names down. Click on each one individually and see if there is autos fill for the password. A lot of people hate constantly having to fill the information in, so they have the site just remember it for them. When one is filled in, just click enters and you can see their e-mail.

Checking E-mails

Do not go through and open new email. That will give you away. Open ones that have already been opened. See what they have read and decided to keep. With all the Spam out there, the new e-mails may just be junk mail; they just did not have time to delete. So do not base an assumption on them. The ones they keep that have been read are important to them. If they are marked with a reply arrow, then you know there is correspondence with the sender. Allow yourself not to slow down. Look for headings that mention memberships, confirmations, or passwords. These are the files you need to open.

Password or site confirmation sites will usually be a greeting letter, but also can provide the id they used and the password that they are using. Write them down; don't try to remember them. E-mails that they are corresponding to, can be opened and read like a book. With most of us just hitting reply all the time, the previous conversations are still there. You may find days or weeks worth of material. You can save the e-mail in a temp file in your main directories that you can save, print, and view later. Print them out then if you need to have them in hand. You must get them secured before a confrontation, or the e-mail may be deleted and trashed.

My files in email boxes can also hold the emails that they really want to keep. Look in them and see what is there. Draft folders and deleted mail are also fair game. Some times the deleted file will require you to re-install the email to the inbox before you can view it. Make sure to delete it when you are done, so it will be back in the deleted file. Comb thought the site and see what you find. Remember a person trying to hide what they are doing, may have multiple email accounts at different servers.

Make sure to look in the trash folder. Like before, if the file was trashed does not mean they asked for it. Look for the suspicious stuff though. You may find pictures or conversations that they really do want to hide. They may be at the level of covering their tracks that the trash may still reveal. They may also be at the level that they empty the trash folder and you see nothing.   Most people are not that ritualistic or consistent.   You will probably find trash in the folder.

The instant messenger or chat forum may also be one of their site features, so try and open it while in their email.   If they have an account it will usually log it on and open it up.   Look at the friend list and pull up profiles.   See who is on the list, where they say they live, etc.   You may find that when you get on line with their id, some one will start trying to chat with you.   DO NOT try and have a chat session with them.   They will figure you out real quick.   Just say hi or that you can't talk back but can listen.   They may fill you in without ever asking.   Getting the id names from the messenger will allow you to try and friend them latter.   You can use a friend approach that they confide in, not knowing you are the other persons partner.

If all pans out this will give you all the evidence you need though the e-mail server.   If the password or id can not be found with this method, then remember the age old one, look for it around the computer area.   Everyone hates to forget their passwords, so chances are it is written down some where.   Under the keyboard, behind the monitor, under the desktop, and the list goes on.   The point is that if it is something that you need at the computer, then it is near the computer.

If access to the computer is a failure then take it to an expert.   Tell them that you cannot remember your passwords.   A little fee and they will give you the information or find it in the computer for you.   Remember to make sure this is a friend or one that a friend uses.   Take the friend with you to help persuade the computer expert to help.   A lot of times they will show you where the passwords are stored and how to access them on your system.

Another tool that can be used on the computer is an

accountability program. These programs store what is done on the computer and can put it in a file for you to view latter, or email the file to a preset destination. The one using the computer doesn't even know it is running. This is actually the easiest and laziest way to get what you are looking for. It will cost you some money. There are many computer tricks that can be pursued, but if these do not work; then you will not catch your cheater by this method. He is obviously smart enough on a computer to cover his tracks.

If dating sites are found, then you can find the site through your Internet id and set them up. Just log onto the site they are using, make an anonymous id and start corresponding to them. Make sure you put in your fake personal information that you are local. If a picture is required then use an odd one from a magazine, just not one of a famous person. Actively try to get their attention in the site mail or message system. Set the meeting up and make it convenient that you going to be out doing something else. Make sure to take a friend, or a person that your partner respects. Then meet them with your evidence and nail them to the wall. Make sure to bring a print out of your chat or e-mails so that they can not try and wiggle out of the situation.

Kids

Children add a whole new level to our lives. Biological, adopted, step, step once removed, and the many other combinations in today's society. Children all have the lack of experience in common. What do I mean? As you grew up, you had to learn everything you did. When the doctor delivered you, you did not know how to write, read, talk, or control your emotions. You used trial and error to develop into your our unique personality and skill sets you use in life today. People develop what they have at different rates, according to the necessity of the moment.

We all know that when you tell a child not to do something, they do it. Children test how far they can push the boundaries in their lives. Learning at an early age what they can and cannot get away with. As adults we either allow children to move this invisible boundary, or we hold children within these boundaries. Children look to adults to establish the order and discipline in their lives. When an adult fails at this task, the child mentally places himself or herself above that adult. They are now in charge of the adult. It is hard to regain the ground lost to a child.

With a little bribing, children keep their mouth shut most of the time. Put fear into them and they may never mention it for as long as they live. The point is that we know as adults that children do not have the discretion to know what is to be overlooked and what needs to be confronted. They learn as they age by trial and error. Some children learn faster than others do. Some children never learn this discretion. Children also learn what may be used as blackmail, to control others. Threatening to tell what was done, to make another submit to their will. If we can remember how we learned in our childhood, then we can learn from our children as well.

"Mommy, mommy, guess what? Daddy bought me a new brats doll today and she's my favorite. She has brown hair and we bought all the accessories. I want to call Janna over so that she can see my new brat doll." Holly exclaims.

"Hold on, I am a little busy, so what did you say?" mom asks.

"I want Janna to come over and play with my brat dolls. She can bring hers over and play with me like we did yesterday" holly retells.

"I don't know if we can have her over today. The house is a mess and I don't feel like cleaning it up today" mom explains

"We can stay in my room and we won't come out and bother you, just like yesterday. We played in Janna's room all afternoon. She has the neatest toys. Guess what she has on her ceiling?" Holly exclaims

"I don't know, what?" mom asks.

"She has a bazzion glow in the dark stars stuck to the ceiling. Can we get some?" Holly asks.

"Maybe. Can she come over tomorrow, so that I have time to clean the house? Maybe you should help since it is your friend that wants to come over." Mom states.

"Daddy will help clean it, he helped clean hers. We heard them even moving the furniture to clean under it." Holly proceeds.

"Really?" mom questions.

"We go over every Tuesday and play. Usually we stay in Janna's room and play. Daddy helps her mom each week, so I am sure he will help clean our house. Just ask him. So can Janna come over? Please, please, please; I want to call her now." Holly begs.

Then he better help clean this one, since he has time to help someone else clean theirs."

Is the mom listening listen to her daughter? You hear what the child is saying. You just aren't listening. Why did daddy go and buy a toy with all the accessories? How come she was playing so long yesterday? Why did they have to stay and Janna's room the whole time? Why did daddy stay the whole time? Why is dad, the guest, cleaning the house? Did you know they go every Tuesday? How often do you move the furniture to clean?   Lots of questions pop out of this conversation.   Maybe he did have to help them move or do some major cleaning.   Mom should have already known, not been surprised.   So if that is the case then mom should have been told by dad yesterday.

This mom never figured it out on her own.   It was more than a year.   Janna was mad at Holly, so yelled out at school that Holly's dad didn't love her mom.   In the middle of their fight, Janna took her knowledge and used it as a weapon. Holly did not know the secret would ever be revealed.   Her and Janna had decided to sneak up on her mom and scare her with a spider.   They found their parents in the middle of sex instead. They went back to Janna's room and promised each other never to tell what they saw.   The yell out was like wild fire.   Kids told friends and family members.   The news was around town before the day was out.   Holly's mom was confronted by friends to see if the rumor was true.   You can already follow that so much damage was done that both relationships ended in divorce.   The two girls ended up separated by distance when families moved apart.

We tell children to stay in their rooms when we do not want them to see something or we are punishing them.   Since we can rule out the punishment, because they were playing; then we can assume that they were not supposed to see something.   Like why the furniture was moving.   Think I am far fetched?   When you pick up the house, don't you try to get the kids to help?   How many men volunteer to go clean someone else's house?   Put those together and you get a suspicious ending.

When people have kids, they have to become creative on how to have sex without the kids knowing.   So we distract the kids, or find somewhere for them to go. Then we can do what we want to do. How many people put a movie in to occupy their child? We know the child glued to the television for an hour and a half? We do it in our homes all the time. A cheater already has the experience needed to deal with children when they want to cheat. The fact that a child is around may be unavoidable for them, so they just make do.

Undeniably is the fact that children are unpredictable. They may not know what you are doing, but they know what they are doing. We just hope that they do not become curious or lonely and start looking for us. Children want us to give approval or disapproval for the things they do. They want you to share in things they like and are doing. They just want to tell you at the time they think of it. They may be interrupting at an inconvenient time and they don't even know it. This is why if we listen to our children we can find out about everything they know. Things done with friends, pets, family, and so on. Things that they were not even trying to tell us.

Children have also been known to get curious. They sneak around and see thing we don't even realize. Curiosity is how they learn. They find Christmas gifts and birthday presents that are hidden. Toys we took away are back in their hands when they want to play. Children have a way of finding things that we don't want them to. How many kids see their first porn experience by finding something their parents thought was hidden? Many times they don't say anything until confronted or made angry.

Children will keep things quiet, if they think they are protecting the person they love. They believe that protecting a loved one is more important than protecting them. How many children live in abuse and stay quiet about it? Most times the children are made to believe that if they tell, then someone else will get hurt from it.   They believe that they will be the one at fault for hurting the loved one.   This lie is more common than you think.

Do not underestimate what you can learn from a child. Just because they are children does not mean they can not teach you.   Learn from what they say.   Learn from what they do. Learn from how they act around others.   Learn their fears and joys.   Children are like an open book.   All we have to do is pay attention enough to read the pages of their lives.

Credit Cards and Receipts

"Honey did you realize the Chinese restaurant charges you for two meals each time you eat there for lunch?" Kim asked.

"No, I had no idea.   What makes you think they do that?" mark replied.

"Well I am looking at the credit card statement and I noticed that when you go to lunch from work, it is about the same price as when we go at night.   I know lunch is a little cheaper than dinner, so they must be charging you twice." Kim states.

"Let me have the statement and I will go in tomorrow and fix it." Mark states.

This is a simple problem right?   How come they charge him wrong ever time?   An error should occur once or twice, not every time.   If it's a computer error, then why does it not make the same mistake at night?   Maybe she just needs to see which days of the week he eats there and pop in for a surprise lunch together.   But then he may have to pay for three meals, probably none of them eaten.

She decided to check on the matter herself.   On the phone the restaurant said that they did not make mistakes like that, and asked why she did not question it when she paid the bill each time.   She then decided to go in person and get the matter resolved.   She decided that she would go when he ate at the restaurant and compare the bill when it was made.   She wanted to prove the restaurant was making the error and get the money credited to the credit card.   When she arrived at the restaurant, she first made sure his car was in the parking lot. She knew he had 1 hour to take a lunch and that he should need to get back to work.   She went in so that she could intercept him with the receipt after he paid his bill.   This way she could prove to the restaurant that they were making the mistake in charging him twice. Her timing was a little off. She walked in as he was approaching the cash register to check out. The problem was that the restaurant was not making a mistake. They charged for two meals because there was two meals ordered. Unless her husband was not paying for the meal of the woman he had his arm around. The restaurant asked them never to return after the scene she made.

We pay for almost everything by some sort of plastic card in today's world. It is easier, faster, and more convenient than writing checks or having to get cash from the bank. This habit can also be overlooked when someone is cheating. Especially if the one that they are with does not know they are cheating. The cheater needs to follow the same normal suit as if he was not attached. A skilled cheater will make sure to carry lots of cash so that they can pay without a paper trail back home.

When cash is used, then the paper trail is on the bank statement. Unidentified withdrawals, unable to figure out where the money went, and cash being used that you don't ever remember getting anything for. The other paper trail is the receipts that are found but that is the only paper trail when cash is used. A paper trail that does not seem important at the time of purchase and that is not always gotten rid of.

A clever cheater will throw out any receipts received for purchase that involve their lover. Problem is that they would have to be methodical in this practice. Receipts will often be mixed with the normal ones. In jackets, cars, stacks of papers, and so on, places where you may find them. Where ever you dump everything else when you are done with it. I don't know how many times I have been busted for buying junk at a convent store when I get my gas.   It's on the receipt with the gas purchase.   Many cluttered people also just drop receipts in the consul of the car, or the floorboard.   Easy enough to pick them up and see what has been purchased.   I mean when you see a dozen roses was purchased at the florist and you never got any, well hmmm, where did they go?

A cheater cannot make enough adjustments to cover up that money is being used to seduce or keep up the one they are cheating with.   The only exception is if they are paying for everything.   But then you have to explain how you paid for your lunch or what money you used to buy that new necklace. To spend or not spend money in a cheating relationship is a no win situation.   If your really want to catch your partner, then this is one area you will find clues, if you want to acknowledge the clue that are found.

Disease

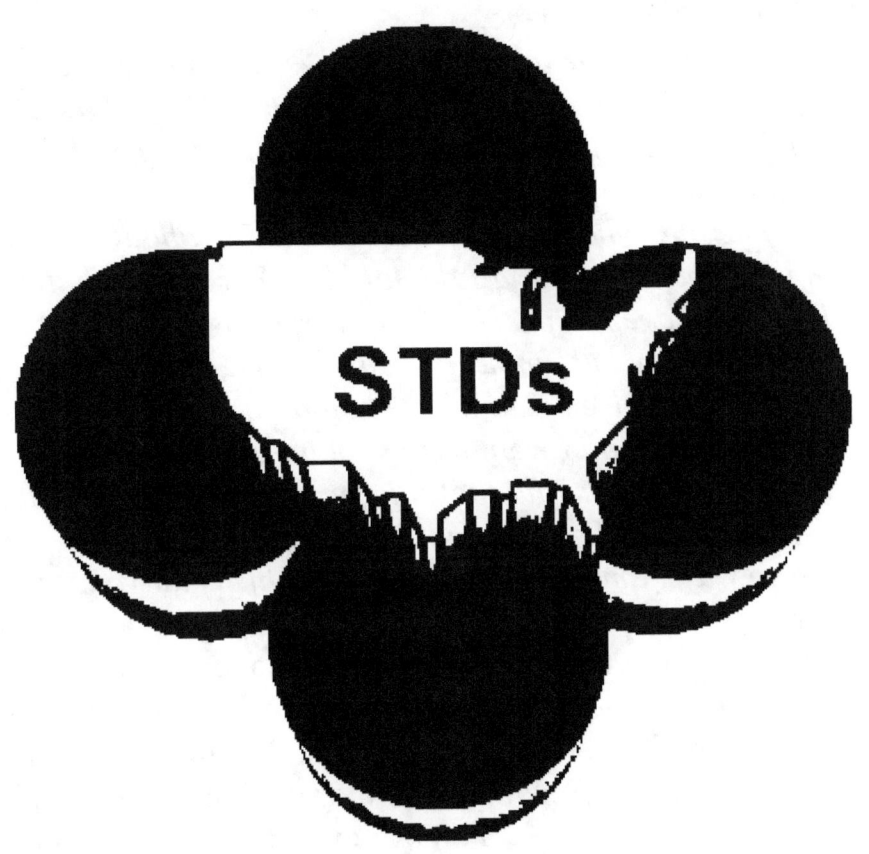

The idea of catching a communicable disease from another person, is enough to keep some people from cheating. Knowing that some one has mono; there is no way I am going to kiss them.   There is no way I am going to have sex with a known AIDS victim.   No one intends to go and catch any disease, so how does it seem to happen?   It is easy, no one asked.   If you do not "see" the disease then you most likely are not going to ask if they have it, and no one is going to come up and tell you what they have.

"Terry, it's your fault I got Herpes.   I know you are running around on me and this is the proof.   Now I have something I can't get rid of and will be with me the rest of my life.   I hate you." Tina yelled

"Time out, what the hell are you talking about?   I am not running around on you and I do not have Herpes.   What makes you think you have Herpes?"   Terry responds

"I know you are running around on me and that you gave this to me.   How else could I have caught it?   The sore down there is irritating and I went to the doctor's office.   They confirmed what it was and that it is very unlikely that I caught it from a toilet seat.   They looked at me like I was a whore, and there is no way I am going back there.   This is all you fault. Stay away from me." Tina sobs.

This guy got no breaks, no defense, and no more sex life. These two are married.   I saved this section for last for multiple reasons.   There is more to cheating than the simple pleasure of sex.   Sometimes, the one nightstand or the long affair can leave an impact on you for life.   You can even pass diseases on to the ones you love, with out even knowing it.

This couple had problems long before this encounter. The wife is very insecure and feels everyone is against her. She has been accusing her husband for years of cheating on her and treating her poorly.   He claims he loves her, does not cheat on her, and treats her as good as he knows how.   Sounds pretty common to a lot of relationships.

After the euphoria of love that got the two of you

together wears off, then reality hits.   How you choose to handle the relationship is what determines how it develops.   It takes work to make relationships work.   This couple didn't learn to communicate with each other, so they did not know how to work together.   This all means that the relationship went stagnant.   Easy to solve, split up.   Problem is that they have kids and do not want the children growing up in a broken home. These settles out to them living together but separate.

When the discovery of herpes came to light, this couple had not had sex in seven months.   Seems like an eternity to me. She was always accusing, directly or indirectly, that he was messing around on her.   She decided that she would no longer be intimate with him because it was not fair that he was not totally committed to her.   Makes since, I mean if they are not going to be faithful then why should we expose our intimate body or emotions.   They will just end up hurting us and we need to set the barrier up so we do not get to hurt.

I learned that about six months after the herpes discovery that Terry did confess to having a one night stand with a co-worker, a year before.   She tried to blackmail him and he almost lost his job over it.   He was scared and never admitted to any of it before, always denying it.   Even his co -workers didn't believe it.   They remembered this girl making very forward and open advances on him and that he would never take her up on her offers.   They thought she got mad and started trying to get back at him for not accepting her.   They remember that it came down to one of them getting fired soon and rightly so it was her.   He was the best worker in the entire group, never late; the one put in charge all the time.   She was relatively new, had a drug problem (no one could seem to catch), and had drama problems all the time.   They never thought an affair ever happened even though most thought he was a nut for not jumping on the opportunity.

Terry's wife dug in hard. She made sure to let everyone know. She told the kids, their parents, co-workers, and the church. He was a whipped dog and she was determined that he was going to pay for what he did, every day for the rest of his life. Terry knew he did wrong and was guilty, so he felt like he was getting what he disserved. He said that when the one nightstand had happened, his wife and him were already having problems. No sex in three months and she keep leaving town with their new son for her mom's. He felt abandoned, now that she finally had a child, which was all she wanted. That she no longer needed him. He felt like he was being used to support the family and getting no benefit for it. This girl at work had been persistent, so he finally took her up on it.

Two more years have passed and a new bomb rocks this broken relationship. Yes, they are still together. Terry is now taking anti-depressants to get through life. He has not had sex with his wife for three and a half years. She has let up, but will only let him have a relationship of friends. Well not quite, he still has to support everybody, since she will not work. The new bomb is that Tina got a notice from the blood bank, she is now longer allowed to give blood. The notice tells her that she needs to go and have blood work done to determine if she has AIDS or a clear test saying she does not. If she brings proof she does not, then they will let her start giving blood again. What should I say?

Terry is really down, he must have gave it her also. Tina is doing nothing but crying, it is the end of life, as she knows it. The blood work shows that she does have AIDS. The doctor asks all sorts of questions and Terry tells of the one nightstand.

He thought a condom would have kept all this from happening. The doctor then takes Terry's blood work to see how advanced it is in him.

Well when the doctor brings them back in, Terry can see he is puzzled. The doctor starts with questions about tattoos, drug use, piercing, accidental needle sticks, if she was raped, and on and on. Everything is no, Terry and Tina are getting irritated. Did the doctor call them in just to grill her? Terry wants to know why all the questions. The doctor sits back and puts the chart down. He says the problem is that Terry does not have AIDS, so she could not have got it from him. He goes on to say that Terry does not have Herpes. He does not even have a cold. Terry is completely clean. He is trying to find out how she caught the disease. He went back in her charts and found the Herpes discovery three years ago, but that's it. The Doctor then looks at Tina and says, "You are lying about something. People do not get AIDS from a toilet seat. So tell me or we cannot figure out the best coarse of action from here."

The truth was reluctantly coming out. Those trips to her mom's, well that was not entirely true. She went there but started to see an old school friend. He said he loved her and could see how unhappy she was. That he would never cheat on her like her husband was. After about a month of this affair and he dumps her. He says it will not work out. He says she is still married and needs to deal with her marriage and then maybe they could be together. Tina tells him that she will divorce her husband so they can be together. He tells her when she has taken care of her own relationship; she can look him up again. She was hurt but decided to go home and leave Terry.

She had to get some baby items for the night before she

headed home, so went to the store.   There was accident on the way to Wal-Mart, so she decided to go to a different one on the other side of town.   She was devastated to find her new lover in the baby section, with his wife and two kids.   She was so shocked; she just stood there.   When her baby started to cry, they looked over.   She said he turned white.   How could he have done that to her.   He said he loved her and that she needed to go home and take care of her marriage.   He is married and cheating with her.   She turned and went straight out the store.   She could hear that his wife did not miss a clue. Apparently he had been caught before.   He claimed she meant nothing to him and that he loved her and the kids.   She couldn't understand the rest as she bolt for the car.   She realized she had been used and that he did not love her as he said.

She rationalized in her mind that this guy was just like her husband.   That he was using other women and saying he loved her.   She was going to catch him and make him pay for doing this to her.   She wanted to make him suffer for being a cheating dog.   He must really not love her.   He was going to pay for that.   He was going to have to live and support his family, while she would never touch him again.   She hated men.

With all this news out on the table, she realized that she was worse than he ever was.   He had a one-night stand and stopped, she had a longer affair and almost left her family.   She said she felt guilty but justified it when Terry finally admitted his one-night stand.   She savored what she thought was justice against him and actually both men.   Now she realized that she was the one to blame.   She neglected her family, looking for the rush of love again.   She did not work on her marriage, but worked to destroy it.   She knows that Terry would have never feel prey to this co-worked, if she had just been there. She caught the disease from her affair. Fact was that Terry never had sex since his one nightstand, so he could not have given it to her.

Now what? Terry has every right to point the finger and condemn his wife. He has the right to shame her to everybody, rub her nose in it all. He has the right to pack it all up and leave. I would have, sorry I would have and so would most of you.

Terry is definitely a different being. He held her in the doctor's office as she cried. He did not reject her, but held her. He decided when he married her that her would always be there for the good and the bad. He had the good for about two years and the rest have been bad, but he was committed. At lest now it was all making sense. People still wonder what the hell he is thinking. They have stayed married for another four years now, and seem truly happy. No they still don't have sex and they know she will eventually die from the disease, but they are happy again.

Catching a disease is a reality in the open sexual society we live in. Have sex with enough different people and you are bound to catch something. If you are lucky you will only catch something that medicine can cure. Catch something serious and you will have it the rest of your life. A life that maybe shorter because of your new disease. Why risk the chance of catching something for a moment of pleasure? It is because the act of sex feels so good to us. We have to remember to continue to think with our brains and not our emotions. We also need to accept the consequences for our actions.

Advice

Catching your cheater is not the end. Now you have to decide how to proceed. Like Terry you can learn to forgive and work on the relationship, or you can destroy all remembrance of the relationship. Whichever choice you make, it will be your choice. Live with your decisions knowing they are the right ones for you. If you decide to work it out, then abstain for sexuality until you have a new foundation under your relationship. Make sure disease has not been brought into the relationship by both being tested right away, and before deciding to have sex again.   Some diseases can take awhile before they can be detected.   If a disease is present, then the two of you will have to address it before you start to become intimate again.   At this point you still have the choice to move forward or apart.   No one else I know than Terry can accept an AIDS victim as a wife.   It would be good to know if there is disease before you take it on blindly.

Take the time to learn why the relationship failed in the first place.   Be honest with each other, find out if this relationship can be reconciled.   Learn each other anew and find out if you really want to be with this person or not.   Is it just the feeling of love or is there a deeper relationship of friendship.   I was told a long time ago that there is a fine line between love and hate.   There is also a large area of grey between friends.   Learn to combine both in order to maintain a lasting relationship.